Going Solo · Flute

first performance pieces for flute with piano
erste Vortragsstücke für Flöte und Klavier
premières pièces de concert pour flûte et piano

Philippa Davies & Paul Reade

© 1995 by Faber Music Ltd
First published in 1995 by Faber Music Ltd
3 Queen Square London WC1N 3AU
Cover illustration by John Levers
Cover design by S & M Tucker
Music processed by Chris and Gail Hinkins
Printed in England by Halstan & Co Ltd

ISBN 0 571 51495 2

FABER *ff* MUSIC

1. Speed, Bonny Boat

Fahr zu, gutes Boot   Va, mon joli bateau

Traditional
arr. Paul Reade

2. Oh Soldier, Soldier

Oh, du Soldat!   Oh soldat, soldat

Traditional
arr. Paul Reade

3. Drifting

Treibend   Partir à la dérive

Paul Reade

4. Birds

Vögel   Les Oiseaux

Paul Reade

5. Screw Loose

Paul Reade

Watch out for the change of quaver groupings from 3 + 2 to 2 + 3 in bars 14 and 18!
Vorsicht in den Takten 14 und 18: die Achtel werden dort statt 3 + 2 zu 2 + 3 gruppiert.
Veillez au changement de groupes de croches (de 3 + 2 à 2 + 3) aux mesures 14 et 18!

6. Papageno

Mozart
(from *The Magic Flute*)
arr. Paul Reade

7. Drinking Song

Trinklied *Chanson à boire*

Verdi
(from *La Traviata*)
arr. Paul Reade

8. Where the Bee Sucks

Thomas Arne
arr. Paul Reade

9. Grande Valse Brillante

Chopin
arr. Paul Reade

Going Solo · Flute

Philippa Davies & Paul Reade

1. Speed, Bonny Boat

Fahr zu, gutes Boot   Va, mon joli bateau

Traditional
arr. Paul Reade

This music is copyright. Photocopying is illegal.

2. Oh Soldier, Soldier

Oh, du Soldat!   Oh soldat, soldat

Traditional
arr. Paul Reade

3. Drifting

Treibend   Partir à la dérive

Paul Reade

4. Birds

Vögel   Les Oiseaux

Paul Reade

4

5. Screw Loose

Paul Reade

Watch out for the change of quaver groupings from 3 + 2 to 2 + 3 in bars 14 and 18!

Vorsicht in den Takten 14 und 18: die Achtel werden dort statt 3 + 2 zu 2 + 3 gruppiert.

Veillez au changement de groupes de croches (de 3 + 2 à 2 + 3) aux mesures 14 et 18!

6. Papageno

Mozart
(from *The Magic Flute*)
arr. Paul Reade

7. Drinking Song

Trinklied   Chanson à boire

Verdi
(from *La Traviata*)
arr. Paul Reade

8. Where the Bee Sucks

Thomas Arne
arr. Paul Reade

9. Grande Valse Brillante

Chopin
arr. Paul Reade

Hydret 05

10. Ragtime Doll

Paul Reade

Steady, with a lilt
(♩ = c.168)   (**2. slower, then gradually getting faster**)

11. Mazurka

Delibes
(from *Coppelia*)
arr. Paul Reade

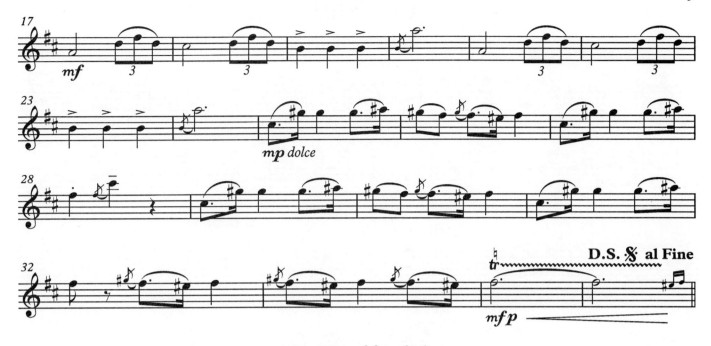

12. Daffodils

Osterglocken   Les narcisses

Paul Reade
(after Billy Mayerl)

13. Waltz
Walzer Valse

Grieg
arr. Paul Reade

14. Wedding Day at Troldhaugen*

Hochzeitstag in Troldhaugen   Jour de noces à Troldhaugen

Grieg
arr. Paul Reade

Tempo di marcia un poco vivace (♩ = c.120)

* Grieg had a country villa at Troldhaugen.
  Grieg hatte ein Landhaus in Troldhaugen.
  Grieg avait une maison de campagne à Troldhaugen.

15. Harvest

Ernte   La Récolte

Paul Reade

10. Ragtime Doll

Tachwedd '05

Paul Reade

11. Mazurka

Delibes
(from *Coppelia*)
arr. Paul Reade

12. Daffodils

Osterglocken   Les narcisses

Paul Reade
(after Billy Mayerl)

13. Waltz

Walzer   Valse

Grieg
arr. Paul Reade

14. Wedding Day at Troldhaugen*

Hochzeitstag in Troldhaugen   *Jour de noces à Troldhaugen*

Grieg
arr. Paul Reade

---

* Grieg had a country villa at Troldhaugen.
Grieg hatte ein Landhaus in Troldhaugen.
Grieg avait une maison de campagne à Troldhaugen.

15. Harvest

Ernte   La Récolte

Paul Reade